ON CHRISTIAN CONTEMPLATION

THOMAS MERTON
ON CHRISTIAN
CONTEMPLATION

Edited, with a preface, by Paul M. Pearson

A NEW DIRECTIONS BOOK

Manufactured in the United States of America
New Directions Books are printed on acid-free paper.
First published as a New Directions Paperbook (NDP1227) in 2012
Design by Erik Rieselbach

Library of Congress Cataloging-in-Publication Data
Merton, Thomas, 1915–1968.
On Christian contemplation / Thomas Merton ; edited, with a preface,
by Paul M. Pearson.
p. cm.
ISBN 978-0-8112-1996-9 (alk. paper) — ISBN 978-0-8112-1997-6
1. Contemplation. I. Pearson, Paul M. II. Title.
BV5091.C7M485 2012
248.3′4—dc23   2012001558

10 9 8 7 6 5 4 3 2 1

New Directions Books are published for James Laughlin
by New Directions Publishing Corporation
80 Eighth Avenue, New York, New York 10011

ndbooks.com

CONTENTS

PREFACE

In a preface to the 1963 Japanese edition of *The Seven Storey Mountain*, Thomas Merton would write that he had never questioned the "definitive decisions" taken in the course of his life—"to be a Christian, to be a monk, to be a priest."[1] Prayer was the life-giving and life-sustaining ground of Thomas Merton's life as a Cistercian monk and priest. His daily life at the Abbey of Gethsemani in rural Kentucky centered on the celebration of the Eucharist, the monastic round of communal, choral prayer seven times a day, *lectio divina*, and personal prayer. In his writings, Merton generally writes of his experience of prayer rather than writing of any methods or techniques he might be using. References to his prayer life are scattered throughout his writings but it is only in a letter of 1966 to a Muslim correspondent in Pakistan, Abdul Aziz, that Merton writes in any detail about his personal spiritual life. In this letter Merton begins by describing the rhythm of his prayer life in his hermitage in the Gethsemani woods— the recitation of the canonical offices of psalms, medi-

1. Thomas Merton, *Honorable Reader: Reflections on My Work*, ed. Robert E. Daggy (New York: Crossroad, 1989), 63.

tation, spiritual reading and celebrating Mass. He then speaks more specifically of his time of meditation writing:

> Strictly speaking I have a very simple way of prayer. It is centered entirely on attention to the presence of God and to His will and His love. That is to say that it is centered on *faith* by which alone we can come to know the presence of God. One might say this gives my meditation the character described by the Prophet as "being before God as if you saw Him" ... it is a matter of adoring Him as invisible and infinitely beyond our comprehension, and realizing Him as all ... such is my ordinary way of prayer or meditation. It is not "thinking about" anything, but a direct seeking of the Face of the Invisible, which cannot be found unless we become lost in Him who is Invisible.[2]

Evident in Merton's writings, and in line with traditional Christian teaching, is the view that there are a variety of forms of prayer, but the ultimate end of these forms should be contemplation, as "contemplation is the highest expression of a man's intellectual and spiritual life."[3] The main forms of prayer which can be found in his writings are liturgical prayer, *lectio divina*, work, meditation and contemplation. Of all these areas Merton devoted his most explicit attention to meditation and contemplation as he saw these as essential for a person to

2. *The Hidden Ground of Love: The Letters of Thomas Merton on Religious Experience and Social Concerns*, ed. William H. Shannon (New York: Farrar, Straus and Giroux, 1985), 62–64.

3. Thomas Merton, *New Seeds of Contemplation* (New York: New Directions, 1961), 1.

obtain union with God and with his or her true self, and believed they were central to the monastic life.[4]

In his glossary to *The Waters of Siloe* Merton defined meditation as follows: "Meditation ... A process which aims to bring the soul to a closer union with God by means of thought, reflection and affective activity of the mind and will, cooperating with ordinary grace."[5] Meditation, in Merton's understanding of it, was not infrequently the beginning of contemplation. Merton believed that meditation was the best method of prayer for the greatest number of people. Nowhere in his writings does he describe techniques and methods of meditation as he believed that there were already sufficient books written on these subjects, and that these books were often misused.

Merton believed that meditation had to have a firm basis in life. Many of his own written meditations in his journals are firmly rooted in his life in the monastery and the surrounding countryside:

Real spring weather—these are the precise days when everything changes. All the trees are fast beginning to be in leaf and the first green freshness of a new summer is all over the hills. Irreplaceable purity of these few days chosen by God as His sign![6]

4. An excellent overview of the various forms of prayer used by Thomas Merton is "Meditation and Prayer in Merton's Spirituality" by John F. Teahan, *American Benedictine Review* 30 (1979), 107–33.
5. Thomas Merton, *The Waters of Siloe* (New York: Harcourt Brace, 1949), 363–64.
6. Thomas Merton, *Dancing in the Water of Life: Seeking Peace in the Hermitage*, ed. Robert E. Daggy (San Francisco: Harper Collins, 1997), 99.

In *New Seeds of Contemplation* Merton proposes a twofold function for meditation. First it teaches each of us how to work ourselves "free of created things and temporal concerns," and secondly it teaches each of us "how to become aware of the presence of God" and bring ourselves to "a state of almost constant loving attention to God, and dependence on Him"[7] moving, he would say, from the false self to the true self.

The Christian mystical tradition generally speaks of two forms of contemplation—active contemplation and passive or infused contemplation. Active contemplation is really the same as Merton's definition of meditation. Active contemplation would prepare each of us for the possibility of occasions of infused contemplation by teaching us how to separate ourselves from falsity, and how to see God's presence in our lives and in the world. In *The Waters of Siloe* Merton defines infused contemplation as "a simple intuition of God, produced immediately in the soul by God Himself, and giving the soul a direct but obscure and mysterious experiential appreciation of God as He is in Himself"[8]—being before God as if you saw Him. Merton's view of contemplation relies heavily on the desert fathers and mothers, the Fathers of the Church, and the great Christian mystics, frequently interpreting those earlier works and making them accessible to a new generation of readers.

Merton saw contemplation as the mark of a completely mature Christian life. It was the reason why

7. Merton, *New Seeds of Contemplation*, 217.
8. Merton, *Waters of Siloe*, 361.

people had been created by God, and it was the highest and most essential of all humanity's spiritual activities prior to the beatific vision. He clearly states this in *New Seeds of Contemplation* where he says of contemplation that it is "life itself, fully awake, fully active, fully aware that it is alive."[9] For Merton contemplation was both a gift infused by God into the soul, and a gift that a person could work and pray for. Infused contemplation is only given to the soul in proportion as it empties itself of all its false concerns through meditation.

In finding God through contemplation we discover our true self and that God is at the deepest core of our being. Integral to discovering God at our true center is the simultaneous discovery that the God we have discovered is love. By emptying ourselves we learn to love God for God's own sake. In an embrace of love we become one with God in love, our soul "is in love, and it knows it is in love, and knows that it is loved in return."[10] In love, and by the power of the Holy Spirit, each of us is transformed so that we become another Christ, as Merton wrote in *The Ascent to Truth* "contemplation is the fullness of the Christ-life in the soul."[11] Each of us as a child of God must then live our lives like the Christ with whom we are one, and the characteristic of the love through this union, is that it is selfless. So our life of union with God through contemplation demands a life of more perfect and more

9. Merton, *New Seeds of Contemplation*, 1.

10. Thomas Merton, *The Ascent to Truth* (New York: Harcourt Brace, 1951), 277.

11. Ibid., 13.

loving actions. As well as loving the God whom we cannot see, we must love our sisters and brothers whom we can see and this love is expressed in our actions towards them.

We can see this change gradually happening in Merton himself as he moved from the world denying monk of his early years in the monastery, who "spurned New York, spat on Chicago, and tromped on Louisville, heading for the woods with Thoreau in one pocket, John of the Cross in another, and holding the Bible open at the Apocalypse,"[12] to the world affirming monk of the final decade of his life who would see all people "shining like the sun,"[13] and could declare: "I love beer, and, by that very fact, the world."[14]

Interior contemplation and exterior action seem paradoxical ideas but Merton finds them intrinsically connected. It is Merton's understanding of this unity that makes his writing so relevant for us today. He sees contemplation and action in loving our brothers and sisters as two aspects of our love for God:

> Action and contemplation now grow together into one life and one unity. They become two aspects of the same thing. Action is charity looking outward to other people, and contemplation is charity drawn inward to its own divine source.[15]

12. Thomas Merton, *Contemplation in a World of Action* (Garden City, NY: Doubleday, 1971), 143.

13. Thomas Merton, *Conjectures of a Guilty Bystander* (Garden City, NY: Doubleday, 1966), 141.

14. Merton, *Contemplation in a World of Action*, 144.

15. Thomas Merton, *No Man is an Island* (New York: Harcourt Brace, 1955), 70.

Each of our actions should proceed from a union with God in prayer; the strength of our actions will depend on the strength of our unity with God: "for union with God in action demands a strong union with Him in prayer."[16] The view of contemplation that Merton presents does not intend for us to forsake our humanity, on the contrary it requires a deepening of our humanity. Through contemplation each of us can deepen our own self-understanding, freedom, integrity, and capacity to love so that our actions will be genuine and not ego-centered. In *No Man is an Island* Merton compares action to a stream and contemplation to the spring, and in this image the spring is essential and the stream will be the result. Thus contemplation should penetrate and enliven all the areas of our lives including the temporal and transient areas.

When we find God as our true center by means of contemplation then our entire lives are totally altered and each of our actions and contemplation will be a mirror of Christ's, as we have each now truly become a child of God.

Merton does not teach anyone to pray. All he does is record his own experiences of prayer. What he has written is a map of his own journey and "any explorer knows that the map is not the journey."[17] In his view knowledge of prayer cannot be taught. It must be gained by experience as he writes in *Spiritual Direction and Meditation*,

16. John J. Higgins, *Thomas Merton on Prayer* (Garden City, NY: Doubleday Image Books, 1975), 96.

17. B. H. Hawker, "Twice Twenty-seven Plus Ten," *Cistercian Studies* 14 (1979), 192.

"the only way to find out anything about the joys of contemplation is *by experience*."[18] Or again, in a talk from 1968, he asks the question: "What is keeping us back from living lives of prayer? Perhaps we don't really want to pray. This is the thing we have to face."[19]

This little volume brings together some pertinent writings of Thomas Merton on meditation and contemplation, including some more obscure pieces from the final months of his life. Its purpose is to encourage the reader on their spiritual journey and, for those new to the work of Thomas Merton, to open up some of the insights of this modern spiritual master. It should not be read as a manual or textbook on the life of prayer but as a "primer" on meditation and contemplation to be read, as Merton himself suggests, "quietly" and "in such a way that when you get something to chew on you stop and chew" in the manner of *lectio divina*, spiritual reading. Such a way of prayer "is a good thing to do" Merton writes, and is "very easy and simple."[20] Every journey starts with the first step, so too the life of prayer, as Merton said: "If you want a life of prayer, the way to get it is by praying."[21]

—PAUL M. PEARSON

18. Thomas Merton, *Spiritual Direction and Meditation & What Is Contemplation?* (Wheathampstead, Herts.: Anthony Clarke, 1975), 94.

19. Quoted by David Steindl-Rast in "Man of Prayer," *Thomas Merton Monk: A Monastic Tribute*, ed. Patrick Hart (New York: Sheed and Ward, 1974), 85.

20. *Thomas Merton in Alaska: The Alaskan Conferences, Journals, and Letters* (New York: New Directions, 1989), 82.

21. Steindl-Rast, "Man of Prayer," 79.

Abbot Lot came to Abbot Joseph and said:

Father, according as I am able, I keep my little rule, and my little fast, my prayer, meditation and contemplative silence; and according as I am able I strive to cleanse my heart of thoughts: now what more should I do?

The elder rose up in reply and stretched out his hands to heaven, and his fingers became like ten lamps of fire. He said:

Why not be totally changed into fire?

The Wisdom of the Desert, 50

MERTON'S CALL
TO CONTEMPLATION

Can contemplation still find a place in the world of technology and conflict which is ours? Does it belong only to the past? The answer to this is that, since the direct and pure experience of reality in its ultimate root is man's deepest need, contemplation must be possible if man is to remain human. If contemplation is no longer possible, then man's life has lost the spiritual orientation upon which everything else—order, peace, happiness, sanity—must depend. But true contemplation is an austere and exacting vocation. Those who seek it are few and those who find it fewer still. Nevertheless, their presence [bears] witness to the fact that contemplation remains both necessary and possible....

Man has an instinctive need for harmony and peace, for tranquility, order, and meaning. None of those seem to be the most salient characteristics of modern society. A book written in a monastery where the traditions and rites of a more contemplative age are still alive and still practised, could not help but remind men that there had once existed a more leisurely and more spiritual way of life—and that this was the way of their ancestors. Thus even into the confused pattern of Western life is woven a certain memory of contemplation. It is a memory so vague and so remote that it is hardly understood, and yet it can awaken the hope of recovering inner peace. In this hope, modern man can perhaps entertain, for a brief time, the dream of a contemplative life and of a higher spiritual state of quiet, of rest, of untroubled joy. But a sense of self-deception and guilt immediately awakens a reaction of despair, disgust, a rejection of the dream and a commitment to total activism. We must face the fact that the mere thought of contemplation is one which deeply troubles the person who takes it seriously. It is so contrary to the modern way of life, so apparently alien, so seemingly impossible, that the modern man who even considers it finds, at first, that his whole being rebels against it. If the ideal of inner peace remains attractive, the demands of the way to peace seem to be so exacting and so extreme that they can no longer be met. We would like to be quiet, but our restlessness will not allow it. Hence we believe that for us there can be no peace except in a life filled up with movement and activity, with speech, news, communication, recreation, distraction. We seek the meaning of our life in activity for its own sake, activity without objective, efficacy without fruit, scientism, the cult of unlimited power, the service of the machine as an end in itself. And in all these a certain dynamism is imagined. The life of frantic activity is invested with the noblest of qualities, as if it were the whole end and happiness of man: or rather as if the life of man had no inherent meaning whatever and that it had to be given a meaning from some external source, from a society engaged in a gigantic communal effort to raise man above himself. Man is indeed called to transcend himself. But do his own efforts suffice for this?

The reason for this inner confusion and conflict is that our technological society has no longer any place in it for wisdom that seeks truth for its own sake, that seeks the fullness of being, that seeks to rest in an intuition of the very ground of all being. Without wisdom, the apparent opposition of action and contemplation, of work and rest, of involvement and detachment, can never be resolved. Ancient and traditional societies, whether of Asia or of the West, always specifically recognized "the way" of the wise, the way of spiritual discipline in which there was at once wisdom and method, and by which, whether in art, in philosophy, in religion, or in the monastic life, some men would attain to the inner meaning of being, they would *experience* this meaning for all their brothers, they would so to speak bring together in themselves the divisions or complications that confused the life of their fellows. By healing the divisions in themselves they would help heal the divisions of the whole world. They would realize in themselves that unity which is at the same time the highest action and the purest rest, true knowledge and selfless love, a knowledge beyond knowledge in emptiness and unknowing; a willing beyond will in apparent non-activity. They would attain to the highest striving in the absence of striving and of contention.

This way of wisdom is no dream, no temptation and no evasion, for it is on the contrary a return to reality in its very root. It is not an escape from contradiction and confusion for it finds unity and clarity only by plunging into the very midst of contradiction, by the acceptance of emptiness and suffering, by the renunciation of the passions and obsessions with which the whole world is "on fire". It does not withdraw from the fire. It is in the very heart of the fire, yet remains cool, because it has the gentleness and humility that come from self-abandonment, and hence does not seek to assert the illusion of the exterior self....

Thus, far from wishing to abandon this way, the author seeks only to travel further and further along it. This journey without maps leads him into rugged mountainous country where there are often mists and storms and where he is more and more alone. Yet at the same time, ascending the slopes in darkness, feeling more and more keenly his own emptiness, and with the winter wind blowing cruelly through his now tattered garments, he meets at times other travelers on the way, poor pilgrim as he is, and as solitary as he, belonging perhaps to other lands and other traditions. There are of course great differences between them, and yet they have much in common. Indeed, the author of this book can say that he feels himself much closer to the Zen monks of ancient Japan than to the busy and impatient men of the West, of his own country, who think in terms of money, power, publicity, machines, business, political advantage, military strategy—who seek, in a word, the triumphant affirmation of their own will, their own power, considered as the end for which they exist. Is not this perhaps the most foolish of all dreams, the most tenacious and damaging of illusions?

In any event, it is certain that the way of wisdom is not an evasion. Simply to evade modern life would be a futile attempt to abdicate from its responsibilities [while clinging to its advantages. The way of contemplation is a way of higher and more permanent responsibilities] and a renunciation of advantages—and illusions. The contemplative way requires first of all and above all renunciation of this obsession with the triumph of the individual or collective will to power.... The life of the collective mass is such that it destroys in man the inmost need and capacity for contemplation. It dries up the living springs of compassion and understanding. It perverts the creative genius and destroys the innocent vision that is proper to man in communion with nature. Finally the collective mass becomes a vast aggregate of organized hatred, a huge and organized death-wish, threatening its own existence and that of the entire human race.

The mission of the contemplative in this world of massive conflict and collective unreason is to seek the true way of unity and peace, without succumbing to the illusion of withdrawal into a realm of abstraction from which unpleasant realities are simply excluded by the force of will. In facing the world with a totally different viewpoint, he maintains alive in the world the presence of a spiritual and intelligent consciousness which is the root of true peace and true unity among men. This consciousness certainly accepts the fact of our empirical and individual existence, but refuses to take this as the basic reality. The basic reality is neither the individual, empirical self nor an abstract and ideal entity which can exist only in reason. The basic reality is being itself, which is one in all concrete existents, which shares itself among them and manifests itself through them. The goal of the contemplative is, on its lowest level, the recognition of this splendor of being and unity—a splendor in which he is one with all that is. But on a higher level still, it is the transcendent ground and source of being, the not-being and the emptiness that is so called because it is absolutely beyond all definitions and limitation. This ground and source is not simply an inert and passive emptiness, but for the Christian it is pure act, pure freedom, pure light. The emptiness which is "pure being" is the light of God which, as St. John's Gospel says, "gives light to every man who comes into the world." Specifically, the Gospel sees all being coming forth from the Father, God, in His Word, who is the light of the world. "In Him (the Word) was life, and this life was Light for all men, and the Light shone in darkness and the darkness could not understand it." (John 1: 4–5)

Now very often the ordinary active and ethical preoccupations of Christians make them forget this deeper and more contemplative dimension of the Christian way. So active, in fact, has been the face presented by Christianity to the Asian world that the hidden contemplative element of Christianity is often not even suspected at all by Asians. But without the deep root of wisdom and contemplation, Christian action would have no meaning and no purpose.

The Christian is then not simply a man of good will, who commits himself to a certain set of beliefs, who has a definite dogmatic conception of the universe, of man, and of man's reason for existing. He is not simply one who follows a moral code of brotherhood and benevolence with strong emphasis on certain rewards and punishments dealt out to the individual. Underlying Christianity is not simply a set of doctrines about God considered as dwelling remotely in heaven, and man struggling on earth, far from heaven, trying to appease a distant God by means of virtuous acts. On the contrary Christians themselves too often fail to realize that the infinite God is dwelling within them, so that He is in them and they are in Him. They remain unaware of the presence of the infinite source of being right in the midst of the world and of men. True Christian wisdom is therefore oriented to the experience of divine Light which is present in the world, the Light in whom all things are, and which is nevertheless unknown to the world because no mind can see or grasp its infinity. "He was in the world and the world was made by Him and the world did not know Him. He came into His own and His own did not receive Him." (John 1: 10–11)

Contemplative wisdom is then not simply an aesthetic extrapolation of certain intellectual or dogmatic principles, but a living contact with the Infinite Source of all being, a contact not only of minds and hearts, not only of "I and Thou," but a transcendent union of consciousness in which man and God become, according to the expression of St. Paul "one spirit."

Though this contemplative union is an extreme intensification of conscious awareness, a kind of *total awareness*, it is not properly contained or signified in any particular vision, but rather in non-vision which attains the totality of meaning beyond all limited conceptions, by the surrender of love. God Himself is not only pure being but also pure love, and to know Him is to become one with Him in love. In this dimension of Christian experience, the Cross of Christ means more than the juridical redemption of man from the guilt of evil-doing. It means the passage from death to life and from nothingness to fullness, or to fullness in nothingness. Thus the contemplative way of ancient Christian monastic tradition is not simply a way of emptiness and transcendence in union with the crucified Christ. The Cross signifies that the sacrificial death which is indeed the destruction of the empirical bodily existence and end of all lust for earthly power and all indulgence of passion, is in fact the liberation of those who have renounced this exterior self in order to dedicate their lives to love and to truth. Christ is not simply an object of love and contemplation whom the Christian considers with devout attention: He is also "the way, the truth and the life" so that for the Christian to be "on the way" is to be "in Christ" and to seek truth is to walk in the light of Christ. "For me to live," says St. Paul, "is Christ. I live, now not I, but Christ lives in me."

This is a summary outline of the meaning of Christian contemplation, a meaning which calls for much greater development particularly in all that concerns the sacramental and liturgical life of the Church.

Such is the way of contemplation that is the subject of this book. But the book is not a systematic treatise. It is only a collection of intuitions and hints, which seek rather to suggest than to define. Nowhere do they claim to present a systematic philosophy or theology, still less an apologetic for Christian ideas.

To read this book one does not need to be a Christian: it is sufficient that one is a man, and that he has in himself the instinct for truth, the desire of that freedom from limitation and from servitude to external things which St. Paul calls the "servitude of corruption" and which, in fact, holds the whole world of man in bondage by passion, greed, the lust for sensation and for individual survival, as though one could become rich enough, powerful enough and clever enough to cheat death.

Unfortunately, this passion for unreality and for the impossible fills the world today with violence, hatred, and indeed with a kind of insane and cunning fury which threatens our very existence.

Science and technology are indeed admirable in many respects and if they fulfill their promises they can do much for man. But they can never solve his deepest problems. On the contrary without wisdom, without the intuition and freedom that enable man to return to the root of his being, science can only precipitate him still further into the centrifugal flight that flings him, in all his compact and uncomprehending isolation, into the darkness of outer space without purpose and without objective.

Preface to the Japanese edition
of *New Seeds of Contemplation*

HOW LONG WE WAIT

How long we wait, with minds as quiet as time,
Like sentries on a tower.
How long we watch, by night, like the astronomers.

Heaven, when will we hear you sing,
Arising from our grassy hills,
And say: "The dark is done, and Day
Laughs like a Bridegroom in His tent, the lovely sun,
His tent the sun, His tent the smiling sky!"

How long we wait with minds as dim as ponds
While stars swim slowly homeward in the water of our west!
Heaven, when will we hear you sing?

How long we listened to the silence of our vineyards
And heard no bird stir in the rising barley.
The stars go home behind the shaggy trees.
Our minds are grey as rivers.

O earth, when will you wake in the green wheat,
And all our Trappist cedars sing:
"Bright land, lift up your leafy gates!
You abbey steeple, sing with bells!
For look, our Sun rejoices like a dancer
On the rim of our hills."

In the blue west the moon is uttered like the word:
    "Farewell."

TOOLS FOR CONTEMPLATION

A THEOLOGY OF PRAYER

A theology of prayer has to be seen in the light of our destiny. What are we here for? What does God intend for His world and for the men He has placed in it? And, since our destiny is fraught with conflict and contradiction and struggle, and even confusion, a theology of prayer is something that must flower in the midst of this struggle and confusion and even personal anguish.

A theology of prayer is a theology which arises in the midst of contradiction. It reminds me of a Zen Buddhist saying: "The way to advance in prayer is to advance head-first into the middle of contradiction." A theology of prayer, therefore, has to be something other than a system which attempts to explain away these contradictions which rack the heart of man, or even attempts to make them intelligible, because they are beyond intelligibility in some cases.

A theology of prayer must give the human spirit support in a struggle which is sometimes intolerable. And I do not mean that the struggle is really tolerable. On the contrary, it is a theology of the cross and the cross was intolerable.

How does the theology of prayer approach this problem? Not by reasoning but by symbol, by poetic insight, leading directly to those depths of the heart where these matters are experienced and where such conflicts are resolved. What we can gain from a theology of prayer is the capacity to experience contradictions and struggles and sufferings as a sharing in the cross. It is not a question of just saying it is a sharing in the cross, but of experiencing it in the deepest possible religious and existential manner, as Christ suffering in us. This cannot be done without passion. A theology of prayer is going to have to be a passionate theology—a theology of *bhakti* we might say ...

Prayer aspires to an immediate relationship with God, a face to face unmediated vision of God. What do we mean by an unmediated approach to God? ... What about the idea of a mediator in prayer? Certainly we do all things through the mediatorship of Christ, but there is a kind of interiorization that has to take place in prayer in which there is no longer I, mediator, and God-beyond-mediator, but in which it is all telescoped and in which Christ the mediator becomes so interiorized in me that He and I are one and my prayer is therefore His prayer.

Progress in prayer is arrived at by this theological telescoping in which the mediator and I become one. He is still obviously mediator—He is still Savior and Christ, but my prayer is now His. We have to dare to make this kind of *rapprochement*, to come close in this way and we have to beware, then, of a theology of prayer that consistently keeps everything at arm's length. If we do that we end up with a theology of prayer which keeps man from God instead of bringing Him closer.

God is jealous of this relationship and we tend to make Him seem jealous of the distance. It is true that He is transcendent. Certainly He is above all and everything, but He is jealous not of that distance but of our coming close to Him. He wants us near to Him. In a certain sense He wants the sinner near to Him even in his sin. That is the meaning of Job. Job is someone who is in trouble, suffering, who dares to come close to God and challenge Him on the issue rather than doing what we all do — as soon as we experience trouble and suffering we go and hide from God. This is the sign of original sin, this is what Adam did. As soon as he got into trouble he didn't pray — he hid. The instinct of man to hide from God has to be considered in a theology of prayer.

There is a passion in the absolute seriousness of God's love for us — the passion you find in the *Song of Songs*, for example. You find it in the words of one of the mystics, Angela of Foligno ... Our Lord said to Blessed Angela of Foligno: "I did not love you as a joke. I was not kidding when I loved you." And this is the very heart of all God's statements in Revelation. The whole Bible is a way of God saying "I was not fooling when I loved you. I was not kidding when I was nailed to the Cross. I was not just putting on an act. This was real." ...

I would like to take the final chapter of St. Luke as an illustration of the New Testament theology of prayer in practice. This is the teaching of Our Lord Himself on prayer, in the context of the New Testament in which the Law has been nailed to the Cross and defeated, along with the enemies of Christ:

> That very day two of them were going to a village named Emmaus, about seven miles from Jerusalem, and talking with each other about all these things that had happened. While they were talking and discussing together, Jesus Himself drew near and went with them. But their eyes were kept from recognizing Him. And He said to them, "What is this conversation which you are holding with each other as you walk?" And they stood still, looking sad. Then one of them, named Cleopas, answered Him, "Are you the only visitor to Jerusalem who does not know the things that have happened there in these days?" (Luke 23: 13–18 RSV)

And you know the rest of the story . . .

This is Job in a very low tone. They are complaining. Our Lord has been crucified. "Don't you know this—don't you know that everything we had hoped for has collapsed? Don't you see that everything has gone wrong?"

> And He said to them, "O foolish men, and slow of heart to believe all that the prophets have spoken! Was it not necessary that the Christ should suffer these things and enter into His glory?" And beginning with Moses and all the prophets, He interpreted to them in all the scriptures the things concerning Himself. (Luke 24: 25–27 RSV)

The whole theology is in that line.

So they drew near to the village to which they were going. He appeared to be going further, but they constrained Him, saying, "Stay with us, for it is toward evening and the day is now far spent." So He went in to stay with them. When He was at table with them, He took the bread and blessed, and broke it, and gave it to them. And their eyes were opened and they recognized Him; and he vanished out of their sight. They said to each other, "Did not our hearts burn within us while He talked to us on the road, while He opened to us the scriptures?" And they rose that same hour and returned to Jerusalem; and they found the eleven gathered together and those who were with them, who said, "The Lord has risen indeed, and has appeared to Simon!" Then they told what had happened on the road, and how He was known to them in the breaking of the bread. (Luke 24: 28–35 RSV)

There is your theology of prayer according to the New Testament. It starts with Job in a low key, suffering, baffled, frustrated, peeved, fully at grips with the problem posed by the fact that the bottom had dropped out of everything they had lived for. At this point a stranger appears and they don't understand why He fails to see their difficulty. They don't know who He is.

The theology of prayer begins when we understand that we are in trouble, and that we have a Savior with us whom we do not recognize. Gradually the meaning of the Gospel begins to be clear to us, and then our hearts burn within us as they witness that reality. As St. Paul says: "The Spirit within our heart cries out to the Father: 'Abba, Father!'" This is the burning within which is the reality of prayer, the response, the recognition that God has accepted us as sons. This is the heart of prayer, the spirit of sonship, consciously responding to God in the awareness of love.

Our Lord goes on to manifest Himself completely to them and then vanishes. This is also part of prayer. The theology of prayer must take into account the point at which Our Lord as a "separate object" vanishes. This has nothing to do with the old controversy about whether or not you should try to imagine the presence of the Lord, because He is present in them, the disciples, in the group that has witnessed His resurrection. From then on that presence cannot be taken away. And there you have the communal dimension of prayer.

The theology of prayer must take into account the resentment of Job, the anger of Job, the frustration and sorrow of the disciples, the constant presence of Christ with those who suffer, the burning of the heart that begins to recognize the spirit of sonship, the disappearance of the visible presence, the consoling presence of Christ. And finally, the awareness that He is always with His Church, and will always be with us as He is with us now at this moment, and will never leave us, and that this promise is unfailing....

[I]t is on this that we should try to build our theology of prayer.

"Toward a Theology of Prayer,"
Cistercian Studies 13 (1978): 191–99

Transcribed by Brother Patrick Hart from a talk given by Thomas Merton on November 25, 1968, at St. Mary's College, Darjeeling, India

Sometimes I don't think we realize that we have the choice of many approaches to prayer. It isn't a question of there being one right way to pray, or one right answer to the question of prayer, and we should be perfectly free to explore all sorts of avenues and ways of prayer....

We may think of ourselves as people who know how to meditate, but the Western Church doesn't really know what meditation is. And, of course, when I say "meditation" I do not mean mental prayer. Mental prayer is only a phrase — you cannot pray with your mind. You pray with your heart or with the depths of your being. The real origin of the expression "mental prayer" was to distinguish it from vocal prayer. If I were to recite the Breviary without moving my lips and without speaking aloud, I would be making mental prayer according to that definition. But mental prayer which would consist of just reasoning things out — that is not prayer. It may be thinking or concentrating, but it is not prayer. As for meditation, we have never really gone into it.

There is, of course, a traditional, simple kind of Christian meditation in the Western Church which has been basically valid from the beginning and is always valid. It is what the Benedictines call *lectio divina*, a special kind of meditative reading, and I think this probably works best and most simply for the majority of people. You take the Bible or some book that means a great deal to you, and you read quietly in such a way that when you get something to chew on you stop and chew. If you want to stop and look out the window, you stop and look out the window. There is nothing wrong with doing that. You may not feel that you are getting anywhere, but it is a good thing to do and very easy and simple.

Thomas Merton in Alaska, 81–82

Learn how to meditate on paper. Drawing and writing are forms of meditation. Learn how to contemplate works of art. Learn how to pray in the streets or in the country. Know how to meditate not only when you have a book in your hand but when you are waiting for a bus or riding in a train. Above all, enter into the Church's liturgy and make the liturgical cycle part of your life — let its rhythm work its way into your body and soul.

New Seeds of Contemplation, 216

Mental prayer is therefore something like a sky-rocket. Kindled by a spark of divine love, the soul streaks heavenward in an act of intelligence as clear and direct as the rocket's trail of fire. Grace has released all the deepest energies of our spirit and assists us to climb to new and unsuspected heights. Nevertheless, our own facilities soon reach their limit. The intelligence can climb no higher into the sky. There is a point where the mind bows down its fiery trajectory as if to acknowledge its limitations and proclaim the infinite supremacy of the unattainable God.

But it is here that our "meditation" reaches its climax. Love again takes the initiative and the rocket "explodes" in a burst of sacrificial praise. Thus love flings out a hundred burning stars, acts of all kinds, expressing everything that is best in man's spirit, and the soul spends itself in drifting fires that glorify the Name of God while they fall earthward and die away in the night wind!

Spiritual Direction and Meditation, 45–46

Meditation is a twofold discipline that has a twofold function.

First it is supposed to give you sufficient control over your mind and memory and will to enable you to recollect yourself and withdraw from exterior things and the business and activities and thoughts and concerns of temporal existence, and second—this is the real end of meditation—it teaches you how to become aware of the presence of God; and most of all it aims at bringing you to a state of almost constant loving attention to God, and dependence on Him.

The real purpose of meditation is this: to teach a man how to work himself free of created things and temporal concerns, in which he finds only confusion and sorrow, and enter into a conscious and loving contact with God in which he is disposed to receive from God the help he knows he needs so badly, and to pay to God the praise and honor and thanksgiving and love which it has now become his joy to give.

The success of your meditation will not be measured by the brilliant ideas you get or the great resolutions you make or the feelings and emotions that are produced in your exterior senses. You have only really meditated well when you have come, to some extent, to realize God. Yet even that is not quite the thing.

After all, anyone who has tried it is aware that the closer you get to God, the less question there can be of realizing Him or anything about Him.

And so, suppose your meditation takes you to the point where you are baffled and repelled by the cloud that surrounds God, "Who maketh darkness His covert." Far from realizing Him, you begin to realize nothing more than your own helplessness to know Him, and you begin to think that meditation is something altogether hopeless and impossible. And yet the more helpless you are, the more you seem to desire to see Him and to know Him. The tension between your desires and your failure generate in you a painful longing for God which nothing seems able to satisfy.

Do you think your meditation has failed? On the contrary: this bafflement, this darkness, this anguish of helpless desire is a fulfillment of meditation. For if meditation aims above all at establishing in your soul a vital contact of love with the living God, then as long as it only produces images and ideas and affections that you can understand, feel and appreciate, it is not yet doing its full quota of work. But when it gets beyond the level of your understanding and your imagination, it is really bringing you close to God, for it introduces you into the darkness where you can no longer think of Him, and are consequently forced to reach out for Him by blind faith and hope and love.

It is then that you should strengthen yourself against the thought of giving up mental prayer; you should return to it at your appointed time each day, in spite of the difficulty and dryness and pain you feel. Eventually your own suffering and the secret work of grace will teach you what to do.

You may perhaps be led into a completely simple form of affective prayer in which your will, with few words or none, reaches out into the darkness where God is hidden, with a kind of mute, half-hopeless and yet supernaturally confident desire of knowing and loving Him.

Or else, perhaps, knowing by faith that He is present to you and realizing the utter hopelessness of trying to think intelligibly about this immense reality and all that it can mean, you relax in a simple contemplative gaze that keeps your attention peacefully aware of Him hidden somewhere in this deep cloud into which you also feel yourself drawn to enter.

From then on you should keep your prayer as simple as possible.

When it becomes possible to meditate again, meditate. If you get an idea, develop it, but without excitement. Feed your mind with reading and the liturgy, and if the darkness of your simple prayer becomes too much of a tension — or degenerates into torpor or sleep — relieve it with a few vocal prayers or simple affections, but do not strain yourself trying to get ideas or feel fervor. Do not upset yourself with useless efforts to realize the elaborate prospects suggested by a conventional book of meditations.

New Seeds of Contemplation, 217–20

I HAVE CALLED YOU (Isaias 43:1)

Do not be afraid
O my people
Do not be afraid
Says the Lord:

I have called you
By your name
I am your Redeemer
You belong to me.

When you cross the river
I am there
I am with you
When your street's on fire
Do not be afraid
O my people
You belong to me.

Bring my sons from afar
Says the Savior
Bring them from that dark country
Bring them glad and free
Says the Lord
They belong to me.

Bring my sons and daughters
From that far country
From their house of bondage

Set them free
Bring them back in glory
Home to me.

Do not be afraid
O my people
I have called you by your name
You belong to me.

1966

DISCOVERING THE TRUE SELF

Christ is King enthroned in our hearts, which means to say His kingdom is not of this world, a kingdom organized on the pattern of domination and submission and control. Christ is King but He does not control by power; further He does not control by law. This is one of the most important and neglected features of the New Testament.

Christ is King but He controls by love. This love is the very root of our own being. Therefore what we are called to do is to live as habitually and constantly as possible with great simplicity on this level of love which proceeds from the depths of our own being where Christ reigns and loves. This is a dimension of life which no one can take away unless we close the door ourselves, and no one can bring it in unless we open the door to Christ, opening our hearts to Christ and dwelling there. Even before the Lord dwells in us by His Spirit there is a deeper presence which comes, in a certain sense, from the fact that we are created in Him and, as we read in Colossians (1:16ff.), live in Him—our being is in Christ even ontologically. God wills us to come into being in

Christ. All things are sustained and maintained in being by Him, in Him, through Him by His love....

Who am I? My deepest realization of who I am is that I am one loved by Christ. This is a very important conception.... The depths of my identity is in the center of my being where I am known by God. I know He sees me. I am glad He sees me, and His seeing is love and mercy and acceptance. The great central thing in Christian faith and hope is the courage to realize oneself and to accept oneself as loved by God even though one is not worthy. Identity does not consist in creating worthiness, because He loves us anyway. We know God loves us as we are. This is a very obscure part of our being, but it is at this level where we pray in God's presence.

Prayer is nothing more than getting down to this level and being known to God and responding in the best way we can to God—praying our prayer with our whole hearts, not trying to pray as someone else, but with our own love, even with our own silence. Then we are above all creatures redeemed by Christ and called to a mission, and this is the thing which sets us face to face with those primitive and more ancient religions with their great variety of ways of approach to God and which are so complex and so rich and so diverse.

This call to respond to Christ is absolutely and totally simple. This simplicity distinguishes Christianity from all other religions but Buddhism (which is not really a religion at all) and, in a sense, Islam. But basically our response to Christ is so simple that it cannot be put into words. It is too simple for words, and in a certain way it is rather difficult to witness to because it is so simple. I think we tend to complicate it in order to show that we do have something rather complex after all, to protest that we are not so simple after all, that there is something to see.

We have to realize the absolute seriousness of Christ's love for us, which led Him to the cross and makes Him our King—this love in which He has given all for us. In our response we must open ourselves absolutely to Him through prayer, a totality of response. If we do not pray, it is because we sometimes hold superstitions, one form being this: "if I give myself up too much to Him, He will give me something too hard which I cannot do." This is not Christian maturity. It presupposes that our Lord is playing tricks with us all the time. We have to get rid of the thought that God is a powerful deceiver.... Do not think God is trying to catch you.

Our true sense of who we are consists entirely in this response to Christ. But the most important thing is that this response is to someone we really do not know. We know Him; yes, we know Him and we don't know Him. We know who He is, the theology and gospel Mystery, and yet we do not really know Him. We respond to someone unknown. We do not like to do this. This is not our way of proceeding. Instead of responding to someone unknown we put in our own picture, readily recognized. It is true, we have to have an idea of Christ. Nevertheless when you get down to the depths of your heart, down to the depths where you pray, these are depths where you are speaking to someone you do not really know. Sometimes He is there and you are so keenly aware of

His tangible presence that you could not doubt who He is; but at other times He is not there for you, and you cannot find Him. It is perhaps at the time when our Lord seems to have abandoned you and it seems impossible he could love you, it is perhaps at this time when He seems most distant that He is closest to you.

If you do not understand this, you give up your prayer when it is most important that you should continue. What do you do then? Wait on the Lord; He will come to you eventually. If we are too involved, too convinced of the necessity and the all-important nature of action, we will neglect these moments and try to do something to forget about it. If the action is necessary it is all right. If it is an escape it is not so all right....

Open yourselves to God.... We are people who stand before the world as witnesses that God does hear us and God will never, never fail us. This is the meaning of our prayer life.

Central to this is the sense of forgiveness as pure gift. We have to really believe that we are totally forgiven and not go about as we used to do, saying that perhaps I will make it to purgatory and perhaps afterwards I will get off a little by indulgences and in a few thousand years I will get to heaven. I am not denying there is a purgatory, but to feel that we have to go through this process is not a fully Christian view of things. It is setting limits. Don't set limits to the mercy of God. Do not believe that because you are not pleasing to yourself you are not pleasing to God. If I am truly sorry then I must be just as open to everybody else. If I hold anything against anybody else, the openness is not true.

There you get the area in which prayer functions. Open up this area and dwell there all the time no matter what you are doing. If we dwell in this dimension it does not matter what we are doing. If it is not recognized by the newspaper, that is irrelevant; that is not the Christian dimension. The Sister in the infirmary who can only sit in a wheel chair may be doing more than the whole congregation. This is a well known truth. God does not ask for results. He asks for love, and this cannot be changed. If we get good results with love that is fine. Love without results—it is even better. Ultimately this brings us to nothing new, but when you remember these things in their proper perspective you solve all the crises of today.

"A Conference on Prayer," *Sisters Today* 41 (1970): 449–56
Transcribed by Brother Patrick Hart and Naomi Burton Stone from a talk given by Thomas Merton on November 25, 1968 in Calcutta, India

The first thing you have to do, before you even start thinking about such a thing as contemplation, is to try to recover your basic natural unity, to reintegrate your compartmentalized being into a coordinated and simple whole and learn to live as a unified human person. This means that you have to bring back together the fragments of your distracted existence so that when you say "I," there is really someone present to support the pronoun you have uttered.

The Inner Experience: Notes on Contemplation, 3–4

The secret of my identity is hidden in the love and mercy of God.

But whatever is in God is really identical with Him, for His infinite simplicity admits no division and no distinction. Therefore I cannot hope to find myself anywhere except in Him.

Ultimately the only way that I can be myself is to become identified with Him in Whom is hidden the reason and fulfillment of my existence.

Therefore there is only one problem on which all my existence, my peace and my happiness depend: to discover myself in discovering God. If I find Him I will find myself and if I find my true self I will find Him.

But although this looks simple, it is in reality immensely difficult. In fact, if I am left to myself it will be utterly impossible. For although I can know something of God's existence and nature by my own reason, there is no human and rational way in which I can arrive at that contact, that possession of Him, which will be the discovery of Who He really is and of Who I am in Him.

That is something that no man can ever do alone. Nor can all the men and all the created things in the universe help him in this work.

The only One Who can teach me to find God is God, Himself, Alone.

New Seeds of Contemplation, 35–36

IN SILENCE

Be still
Listen to the stones of the wall.
Be silent, they try
To speak your

Name.
Listen
To the living walls.
Who are you?
Who
Are you? Whose
Silence are you?

Who (be quiet)
Are you (as these stones
Are quiet). Do not
Think of what you are
Still less of
What you may one day be.
Rather
Be what you are (but who?) be
The unthinkable one
You do not know.

O be still, while
You are still alive,
And all things live around you
Speaking (I do not hear)

To your own being,
Speaking by the Unknown
That is in you and in themselves.

"I will try, like them
To be my own silence:
And this is difficult. The whole
World is secretly on fire. The stones
Burn, even the stones
They burn me. How can a man be still or
Listen to all things burning? How can he dare
To sit with them when
All their silence
Is on fire?"

SILENCE

God is present, and His thought is alive and awake in the fullness and depth and breadth of all the silences of the world. The Lord is watching in the almond trees, over the fulfillment of His words (Jeremias 1:11).

Whether the planes pass by tonight or tomorrow, whether there be cars on the winding road or no cars, whether men speak in the field, whether there be a radio in the house or not, the tree brings forth her blossoms in silence.

Whether the house be empty or full of children, whether the men go off to town or work with tractors in the fields, whether the liner enters the harbor full of tourists or full of soldiers, the almond tree brings forth her fruit in silence.

No Man Is An Island, 272–73

A Christian can realize himself called by God to periods of silence, reflection, meditation, and "listening". We are perhaps too talkative, too activistic, in our conception of the Christian life. Our service of God and of the Church does not consist only in talking and doing. It can also consist in periods of silence, listening, waiting. Perhaps it is very important, in our era of violence and unrest, to rediscover meditation, silent inner unitive prayer, and creative Christian silence....

Positive silence pulls us together and makes us realize who we are, who we might be, and the distance between these two. Hence, positive silence implies a disciplined choice, and what Paul Tillich called the "courage to *be*". In the long run, the discipline of creative silence demands a certain kind of faith. For when we come face to face with ourselves in the lonely ground of our own being, we confront many questions about the value of our existence, the reality of our commitments, the authenticity of our everyday lives....

Not only does silence give us a chance to understand ourselves better, to get a truer and more balanced perspective on our own lives in relation to the lives of others: silence makes us whole if we let it. Silence helps draw together the scattered and dissipated energies of a fragmented existence. It helps us concentrate on a purpose that really corresponds not only to the deeper needs of our own being but also to God's intentions for us.

Love and Living, 38-39, 43

Silence does not exist in our lives merely for its own sake. It is ordered to something else. Silence is the mother of speech. A lifetime of silence is ordered to an ultimate declaration, which can be put into words, a declaration of all we have lived for.

No Man Is An Island, 273

If our life is poured out in useless words we will never hear anything in the depths of our hearts, where Christ lives and speaks in silence. We will never be anything, and in the end, when the time comes for us to declare who and what we are, we shall be found speechless at the moment of the crucial decision: for we shall have said everything and exhausted ourselves in speech before we had anything to say.

No Man Is An Island, 275

SONG: IF YOU SEEK . . .

If you seek a heavenly light
I, Solitude, am your professor!

I go before you into emptiness,
Raise strange suns for your new mornings,
Opening the windows
Of your innermost apartment.

When I, loneliness, give my special signal
Follow my silence, follow where I beckon!
Fear not, little beast, little spirit
(Thou word and animal)
I, Solitude, am angel
And have prayed in your name.

Look at the empty, wealthy night
The pilgrim moon!
I am the appointed hour,
The "now" that cuts
Time like a blade.

I am the unexpected flash
Beyond "yes," beyond "no,"
The forerunner of the Word of God.

Follow my ways and I will lead you
To golden-haired suns,
Logos and music, blameless joys,

Innocent of questions
And beyond answers:

For I, Solitude, am thine own self:
I, Nothingness, am thy All.
I, Silence, am thy Amen!

DIFFICULTIES & DISTRACTIONS

Since contemplation is the union of our mind and will with God in an act of pure love that brings us into obscure contact with Him as He really is, the way to contemplation is to develop and perfect our mind and will and our whole soul. Infused contemplation begins when the direct intervention of God raises this whole process of development above the level of our nature: and then He perfects our faculties by seeming to defeat all their activity in the suffering and darkness of His infused light and love.

But before this begins, we ordinarily have to labor to prepare ourselves in our own way and with the help of His grace, by deepening our knowledge and love of God in meditation and active forms of prayer, as well as by setting our wills free from attachment to created things.

About all these things many books have been written. There are all kinds of techniques and methods of meditation and mental prayer, and it would be hard to begin to talk about them all. That is why I shall talk about none of them except to say that they are all good for those who can use them and everyone who can get profit out of systematic meditation should not fail to do so, as long as he is not afraid to lay the method aside and do a little thinking for himself once in a while.

The trouble with all these methods is not that they are too systematic and too formal: they need to be both these things, and it is good that they are. There is nothing wrong with methods. The trouble lies in the way people use them—or fail to use them.

The purpose of a book of meditations is to teach you how to think and not to do your thinking for you. Consequently if you pick up such a book and simply read it through, you are wasting your time. As soon as any thought stimulates your mind or your heart you can put the book down because your meditation has begun....

There are people who only think of meditating when the book is explicitly called "Meditations." If you called it something else they would assume they were just supposed to read it without attempting to think.

The best thing beginners in the spiritual life can do, after they have really acquired the discipline of mind that enables them to concentrate on a spiritual subject and get below the surface of its meaning and incorporate it into their own lives, is to acquire the agility and freedom of mind that will help them to find light and warmth and ideas and love for God everywhere they go and in all that they do. People who only know how to think about God during fixed periods of the day will never get very far in the spiritual life. In fact, they will not even think of Him in the moments they have religiously marked off for "mental prayer."

New Seeds of Contemplation, 214–16

Prayer and love are really learned in the hour when prayer becomes impossible and your heart turns to stone.

If you have never had any distractions you don't know how to pray. For the secret of prayer is a hunger for God and for the vision of God, a hunger that lies far deeper than the level of language or affection. And a man whose memory and imagination are persecuting him with a crowd of useless or even evil thoughts and images may sometimes be forced to pray far better, in the depths of his murdered heart, than one whose mind is swimming with clear concepts and brilliant purposes and easy acts of love.

New Seeds of Contemplation, 221

About prayer: have you a garden or somewhere that you can walk in, by yourself? Take half an hour, or fifteen minutes a day, and just walk up and down among the flowerbeds with the intention of offering this walk up as a meditation and a prayer to Our Lord. Do not try to think about anything in particular and when thoughts about work, etc. come to you, do not try to push them out by main force, but see if you can't drop them just by relaxing your mind. Do this because you "are praying" and because our Lord is with you. But if thoughts about work will not go away, accept them idly and without too much eagerness with the intention of letting Our Lord reveal His will to you through these thoughts. But do not grab at anything that looks like a light. If it is a "light" it will have its effect without your seizing it forcefully.

The Road to Joy, 195

STRANGER

When no one listens
To the quiet trees
When no one notices
The sun in the pool

Where no one feels
The first drop of rain
Or sees the last star

Or hails the first morning
Of a giant world
Where peace begins
And rages end:

One bird sits still
Watching the work of God:
One turning leaf,
Two falling blossoms,
Ten circles upon the pond.

One cloud upon the hillside,
Two shadows in the valley
And the light strikes home.
Now dawn commands the capture
Of the tallest fortune,
The surrender
Of no less marvelous prize!

Closer and clearer
Than any wordy master,
Thou inward Stranger
Whom I have never seen,

Deeper and cleaner
Than the clamorous ocean,
Seize up my silence
Hold me in Thy Hand!

Now act is waste
And suffering undone
Laws become prodigals
Limits are torn down
For envy has no property
And passion is none.

Look, the vast Light stands still
Our cleanest Light is One!

CONTEMPLATION AND ACTION

The Christian consciousness ... is suffering from a kind of schizoid split due to too much self-analysis and too much abstraction. One form this split takes is the duality between prayer and work, regarded as somehow opposite and incompatible. This is due to very ancient habits of thought, going back particularly to St. Gregory the Great and beyond him to pre-Christian thinkers like Plato. It had some point in days when man and society were homogeneous, entire, and whole. Today, when man is split and sundered and looking desperately for wholeness, to exaggerate the division is a disaster. On the other hand, the practical attempt at "solution" by a simple denial of prayer and a total immersion in work is also a disaster. In fact the problem has not been met and there remains an inner guilt that produces not action but frenzy and desperation. It ends with the accusation of others, resentment, etc....

How to face the problem? Mere emphasis on the truly necessary discipline of prayer and meditation is no longer any good. It may produce a momentary effort at "fervor" followed by a relapse, greater unconscious resentment, etc. Or else the false, crabbed, rigid piety of the willful mind that knows how to keep itself in a straitjacket. Painful to itself and to everyone else too. Deadly...

A new approach is needed. Our aim is not simply a recovery of an old discipline, and old fervor, but the opening out of a new consciousness, a new being, in the Spirit. The only possible answer is a new depth and simplicity of love, and this demands a new self-understanding. A self-understanding somehow free of fear and mistrust, free of suspicion, ready for risk, ready to accept mistakes, even big mistakes, knowing that the Spirit is there to make everything right if we are open and sincere with ourselves and with each other. Then openness to God's word. This openness does not replace prayer or substitute for it, but it makes prayer possible. It lays open our own need and the need of others. If it breaks our hearts, that is good too!

All Christian renewal today must be built first of all on basic human realities and values. In this we can learn from "the world"—not from the official world of power and massive organization, but from the world of the men who really struggle with human problems: doctors, teachers, artists, and so on. I have been reading some notes of a doctor who was also a great poet, notes written in an influenza epidemic when he was run off his feet and was nevertheless working on a long poem about the city he lived in, a poem which became a masterpiece. If Dr. Williams could be an "artist" while driving around to visit his patients (mostly poor people) then we too can be men and women of prayer while doing our work. But the key to this unification is LOVE. Love is the power which unites us in "wholeness". And the realization of our *lack of love* is the motive of true prayer.

However, this is not just a matter of inner feeling. Nor is it a matter of abandoned energy and self-outpouring. Love implies both self-giving and self-withholding so that one retains something of a center from which giving continues to be possible. If there is nothing left for you yourself to stand on, how can you help others, how can you save anyone from his own lostness and desperation? ...

To live a life of prayer in our work is then to seek, in the Spirit, a living adjustment between these various demands of love, and to realize that the adjustment will never be perfectly comfortable . Those who joyfully publicize a perfect solution in this matter are simply trying to convince themselves by convincing others. God does not need either our prayer or our activity. Once we realize that, we can go about both with a spirit of greater freedom and abandonment.

"Notes on Prayer and Action," *Light* 1.2 (1967): 1, 3

One of the paradoxes of the mystical life is this: that a man cannot enter into the deepest center of himself and pass through that center into God, unless he is able to pass entirely out of himself and empty himself and give himself to other people in the purity of a selfless love ...

The more I become identified with God, the more will I be identified with all the others who are identified with Him. His love will live in all of us. His Spirit will be our One Life, the Life of all of us and Life of God. And we shall love one another and God with the same Love with which He loves us and Himself. This love is God Himself.

New Seeds of Contemplation, 64–5

Solitude has its own special work: a deepening of awareness that the world needs. A struggle against alienation. True solitude is deeply aware of the world's needs. It does not hold the world at arm's length.

Conjectures of a Guilty Bystander, 10

Contemplation, at its highest intensity, becomes a reservoir of spiritual vitality that pours itself out in the most telling social action.

"The Contemplative Life: Its Meaning and Necessity," *Dublin Review* 223 (Winter 1949), 32

"Action" is no longer a matter of resigning ourselves to work that seems alien to our life in God: for the Lord Himself places us exactly where He wants us to be and He Himself works in us. "Contemplation" is no longer merely the brief, satisfying interlude of reward in which our works are relieved by recollection and peace. Action and contemplation now grow together into one life and one unity. They become two aspects of the same thing. Action is charity looking outward to other men, and contemplation is charity drawn inward to its own divine source. Action is the stream, and contemplation is the spring. The spring remains more important than the stream, for the only thing that really matters is for love to spring up inexhaustibly from the infinite abyss of Christ and of God.

No Man Is An Island, 70

SONG FOR NOBODY

A yellow flower
(Light and spirit)
Sings by itself
For nobody.

A golden spirit
(Light and emptiness)
Sings without a word
By itself.

Let no one touch this gentle sun
In whose dark eye
Someone is awake.

(No light, no gold, no name, no color
And no thought:
O, wide awake!)

A golden heaven
Sings by itself
A song to nobody.

MEDITATIONS

Everything good that comes to us and happens in prayer is a grace and a gift of God—even the desire to pray at all, and the attempt to pray, is itself a great grace. The mere fact of having an opportunity to pray is something for which we should be deeply grateful. St. Paul says that no one can call upon Jesus as Lord, truly, in his heart, without the grace of the Holy Spirit. Hence we can be certain that merely uttering the Holy Name with love is a pledge of great grace. If we learn to recognize all the little ordinary incidents of prayer as graces from God, and to thank Him humbly for them (not necessarily with a lot of words) we will appreciate the simplest and most ordinary "graces of prayer" …

Ardent aspirations of love sometimes arise in the soul more or less passively carrying it beyond all familiar forms of prayer to burning and inexpressible love for God which cannot express itself in words and for which there are no suitable concepts. This is what Cassian calls the "prayer of fire". In the "flame" of this love all our other desires, yearnings, and aspirations are gathered together in one supreme striving to go out of ourselves in love for God and pay Him the homage of supreme adoration.

"Notes on Meditation"

From the archives of the Thomas Merton Ctr. at Bellarmine University

Solitude is not found so much by looking outside the boundaries of your dwelling, as by staying within. Solitude is not something you must hope for in the future. Rather, it is a deepening of the present, and unless you look for it in the present you will never find it.

The Sign of Jonas, 262

The secret of my identity is hidden in the love and mercy of God.

But whatever is in God is really identical with Him, for His infinite simplicity admits no division and no distinction. Therefore I cannot hope to find myself anywhere except in Him.

Ultimately the only way that I can be myself is to become identified with Him in Whom is hidden the reason and fulfillment of my existence.

Therefore there is only one problem on which all my existence, my peace and my happiness depend: to discover myself in discovering God. If I find Him I will find myself and if I find my true self I will find Him.

The only One Who can teach me to find God is God, Himself, Alone.

New Seeds of Contemplation, 35–36

My chief joy is to escape to the attic of the garden house and the little broken window that looks out over the valley. There in the silence I love the green grass. The tortured gestures of the apple trees have become part of my prayer. I look at the shining water under the willows and listen to the sweet songs of all the living things that are in our woods and fields. So much do I love this solitude that when I walk out along the road to the old barns that stand alone, far from the new buildings, delight begins to overpower me from head to foot and peace smiles even in the marrow of my bones.

The Sign of Jonas, 288

To say that I am made in the image of God is to say that love is the reason for my existence, for God is love.

Love is my true identity. Selflessness is my true self. Love is my true character. Love is my name.

To find love I must enter into the sanctuary where it is hidden, which is the mystery of God. And to enter into His sanctity I must become holy as He is holy, perfect as He is perfect.

New Seeds of Contemplation, 60–61

Beauty of sunlight falling on a tall vase of red and white carnations and green leaves on the altar of the novitiate chapel. The light and dark. The darkness of the fresh, crinkled flower: light, warm and red, all around the darkness. The flower is the same color as blood, but it is in no sense whatever "as red as blood." Not at all! It is red as a carnation. Only that.

This flower, this light, this moment, this silence: *Dominus est*. Eternity. He passes. He remains. We pass. In and out. He passes. We remain. We are nothing. We are everything. He is in us. He is gone from us. He is not here. We are here in Him.

All these things can be said, but why say them?

The flower is itself. The light is itself. The silence is itself. I am myself. All, perhaps, illusion. But no matter, for illusion is the shadow of reality and reality is the grace and gift that underlies all these lights, these colors, this silence. Underlies? Is that true? They are simply real. They themselves are His gift.

Conjectures of a Guilty Bystander, 131

It is God's love that warms me in the sun and God's love that sends the cold rain. It is God's love that feeds me in the bread I eat and God that feeds me also by hunger and fasting. It is the love of God that sends the winter days when I am cold and sick, and the hot summer when I labor and my clothes are full of sweat: but it is God Who breathes on me with light winds off the river and in the breezes out of the wood. His love spreads the shade of the sycamore over my head. . . .

It is God's love that speaks to me in the birds and streams; but also behind the clamor of the city God speaks to me in His judgments, and all these things are seeds sent to me from His will.

New Seeds of Contemplation, 14–17

At the center of our being is a point of nothingness which is untouched by sin and illusion, a point of pure truth, a point or spark which belongs entirely to God, which is never at our disposal, from which God disposes of our lives, which is inaccessible to the fantasies of our own mind or the brutality of our own will. This little point of nothingness and of *absolute poverty* is the pure glory of God in us. It is so to speak His name written in us, as our poverty, as our indigence, as our dependence, as our sonship. It is like a pure diamond, blazing with the invisible light of heaven. It is in everybody, and if we could see it we would see these billions of points of light coming together in the face and blaze of a sun that would make all the darkness and cruelty of life vanish completely.... I have no program for this seeing. It is only given. But the gate of heaven is everywhere.

Conjectures of a Guilty Bystander, 142

I looked up at the clear sky and the tops of the leafless trees shining in the sun and it was a moment of angelic lucidity. I said the Psalms of Tierce with great joy, overflowing joy, as if the land and woods and spring were all praising God through me. Again the sense of angelic transparency of everything: of pure, simple and total light.

A Vow of Conversation: Journals 1964–1965, 127

ADVENT

Charm with your stainlessness these winter nights,
Skies, and be perfect!
Fly vivider in the fiery dark, you quiet meteors,
And disappear.
You moon, be slow to go down,
This is your full!

The four white roads make off in silence
Towards the four parts of the starry universe.
Time falls like manna at the corners of the wintry earth.
We have become more humble than the rocks,
More wakeful than the patient hills.

Charm with your stainlessness these nights in Advent,
    holy spheres,
While minds, as meek as beasts,
Stay close at home in the sweet hay;
And intellects are quieter than the flocks that feed by
    starlight.

Oh pour your darkness and your brightness over all our
    solemn valleys,
You skies: and travel like the gentle Virgin,
Toward the planets' stately setting,

Oh white full moon as quiet as Bethlehem!

THE CONTEMPLATIVE DANCE

The Lord made His world not in order to judge it, not in order merely to dominate it, to make it obey the dictates of an inscrutable and all-powerful will, not in order to find pleasure or displeasure in the way it worked: such was not the reason for creation either of the world or of man.

The Lord made the world and made man in order that He Himself might descend into the world, that He Himself might become Man. When He regarded the world He was about to make He saw His wisdom, as a man-child, "playing in the world, playing before Him at all times." And He reflected, "My delights are to be with the children of men."

The world was not made as a prison for fallen spirits who were rejected by God: this is the gnostic error. The world was made as a temple, a paradise, into which God Himself would descend to dwell familiarly with the spirits He had placed there to tend it for Him.

The early chapters of Genesis (far from being a pseudoscientific account of the way the world was supposed to have come into being) are precisely a poetic and symbolic revelation, a completely *true*, though not literal, revelation of God's view of the universe and of His intentions for man. The point of these beautiful chapters is that God made the world as a garden in which He Himself took delight. He made man and gave to man the task of sharing in His own divine care for created things. He made man in His own image and likeness, as an artist, a worker, *homo faber*, as the gardener of paradise. He let man decide for himself how created things were to be interpreted, understood and used: for Adam gave the animals their names (God gave them no names at all) and what names Adam gave them, that they were. Thus in his intelligence man, by the act of knowing, imitated something of the creative love of God for creatures. While the love of God, looking upon things, brought them into being, the love of man, looking upon things, reproduced the divine idea, the divine truth, in man's own spirit.

As God creates things by seeing them in His own Logos, man brings truth to life in his mind by the marriage of the divine light, in the being of the object, with the divine light in his own reason. The meeting of these two lights in one mind is truth.

But there is a higher light still, not the light by which man "gives names" and forms concepts, with the aid of the active intelligence, but the dark light in which no names are given, in which God confronts man not through the medium of things, but in His own simplicity. The union of the simple light of God with the simple light of man's spirit, in love, is contemplation. The two simplicities are one. They form, as it were, an emptiness in which there is no addition but rather the taking away of names, of forms, of content, of subject matter, of identities. In this meeting there is not so much a fusion of identities as a disappearance of identities. The Bible speaks of this very simply: "In the breeze after noon God came to walk with Adam in paradise." It is after noon, in the declining light of created day. In the free emptiness of the breeze that blows from where it pleases and goes where no one can estimate, God and man are together, not speaking in words, or syllables or forms. And that was the meaning of creation and of Paradise. But there was more.

The Word of God Himself was the "firstborn of every creature." He "in whom all things consist" was not only to walk with man in the breeze after noon, but would also become Man, and dwell with man as a brother.

The Lord would not only love His creation as a Father, but He would enter into His creation, emptying Himself, hiding Himself, as if He were not God but a creature. Why should He do this? Because He loved His creatures, and because He could not bear that His creatures should merely adore Him as distant, remote, transcendent and all-powerful. This was not the glory that He sought, for if He were merely adored as great, His creatures would in their turn make themselves great and lord it over one another. For where there is a great God, then there are also god-like men, who make themselves kings and masters. And if God were merely a great artist who took pride in His creation, then men too would build cities and palaces and exploit other men for their own glory. This is the meaning of the myth of Babel, and of the tower builders who would be "as Gods" with their hanging gardens, and with the heads of their enemies hanging in the gardens.

For they would point to God and say: "He too is a great builder, and has destroyed all His enemies."

(GOD said: I do not laugh at my enemies, because I wish to make it impossible for anyone to be my enemy. Therefore I identify myself with my enemy's own secret self.)

So God became man. He took on the weakness and ordinariness of man, and He hid Himself, becoming an anonymous and unimportant man in a very unimportant place. And He refused at any time to Lord it over men, or to be a King, or to be a Leader, or to be a Reformer, or to be in any way superior to His own creatures. He would be nothing else but their brother, and their counselor, and their servant, and their friend. He was in no accepted human sense an important person, though since that time we have made Him The Most Important Person. That is another matter: for though it is quite true that He is the King and Lord of all, the conqueror of death, the judge of the living and of the dead, the *Pantokrator*, yet He is also still the Son of Man, the hidden one, unknown, unremarkable, vulnerable. He can be killed. And when the Son of Man was put to death, He rose again from the dead, and was again with us, for He said: "Kill me, it does not matter."

Having died, He dies no more in His own Person. But because He became man and united man's nature to Himself, and died for man, and rose as man from the dead, He brought it about that the sufferings of all men became His own sufferings; their weakness and defenselessness became His weakness and defenselessness; their insignificance became His. But at the same time His own power, immortality, glory and happiness were given to them and could become theirs. So if the God-Man is still great, it is rather for our sakes than for His own that He wishes to be great and strong. For to Him, strength and weakness, life and death are dualities with which He is not concerned, being above them in His transcendent unity. Yet He would raise us also above these dualities by making us one with Him. For though evil and death can touch the evanescent, outer self in which we dwell estranged from Him, in which we are alienated and exiled in unreality, it can never touch the real inner self in which we have been made one with Him. For in becoming man, God became not only Jesus Christ but also potentially every man and woman that ever existed. In Christ, God became not only "this" man, but also in a broader and more mystical sense, yet no less truly, "every man."

The presence of God in His world as its Creator depends on no one but Him. His presence in the world as Man depends, in some measure, upon men. Not that we can do anything to change the mystery of the Incarnation in itself: but we are able to decide whether we ourselves, and that portion of the world which is ours, shall become *aware* of His presence, consecrated by it, and transfigured in its light.

We have the choice of two identities: the external mask which seems to be real and which lives by a shadowy autonomy for the brief moment of earthly existence, and the hidden, inner person who seems to us to be nothing, but who can give himself eternally to the truth in whom he subsists. It is this inner self that is taken up into the mystery of Christ, by His love, by the Holy Spirit, so that in secret we live "in Christ."

Yet we must not deal in too negative a fashion even with the "external self." This self is not by nature evil, and the fact that it is unsubstantial is not to be imputed to it as some kind of crime. It is afflicted with metaphysical poverty: but all that is poor deserves mercy. So too our outward self: as long as it does not isolate itself in a lie, it is blessed by the mercy and the love of Christ. Appearances are to be accepted for what they are. The accidents of a poor and transient existence have, nevertheless, an ineffable value. They can be transparent media in which we apprehend the presence of God in the world. It is possible to speak of the exterior self as a mask: to do so is not necessarily to reprove it. The mask that each man wears may well be a disguise not only for that man's inner self but for God, wandering as a pilgrim and exile in His own creation.

And indeed, if Christ became Man, it is because He wanted to be any man and every man. If we believe in the Incarnation of the Son of God, there should be no one on earth in whom we are not prepared to see, in mystery, the presence of Christ.

What is serious to men is often very trivial in the sight of God. What in God might appear to us as "play" is perhaps what He Himself takes most seriously. At any rate the Lord plays and diverts Himself in the garden of His creation, and if we could let go of our own obsession with what we think is the meaning of it all, we might be able to hear His call and follow Him in His mysterious, cosmic dance. We do not have to go very far to catch echoes of that game, and of that dancing. When we are alone on a starlit night; when by chance we see the migrating birds in autumn descending on a grove of junipers to rest and eat; when we see children in a moment when they are really children; when we know love in our own hearts; or when, like the Japanese poet Bashō, we hear an old frog land in a quiet pond with a solitary splash—at such times the awakening, the turning inside out of all values, the "newness," the emptiness and the purity of vision that make themselves evident, provide a glimpse of the cosmic dance.

For the world and time are the dance of the Lord in emptiness. The silence of the spheres is the music of a wedding feast. The more we persist in misunderstanding the phenomena of life, the more we analyse them out into strange finalities and complex purposes of our own, the more we involve ourselves in sadness, absurdity and despair. But it does not matter much, because no despair of ours can alter the reality of things, or stain the joy of the cosmic dance which is always there. Indeed, we are in the midst of it, and it is in the midst of us, for it beats in our very blood, whether we want it to or not.

Yet the fact remains that we are invited to forget ourselves on purpose, cast our awful solemnity to the winds and join in the general dance.

New Seeds of Contemplation, 290–97

WORKS BY THOMAS MERTON CITED

The Ascent to Truth. New York: Harcourt Brace, 1951.

The Collected Poems of Thomas Merton. New York: New Directions, 1977.

Conjectures of a Guilty Bystander. New York: Doubleday, 1966.

Contemplation in a World of Action. New York: Doubleday, 1971.

Dancing in the Water of Life: Seeking Peace in the Hermitage, edited by Robert E. Daggy. San Francisco: Harper Collins, 1997.

The Hidden Ground of Love: The Letters of Thomas Merton on Religious Experience and Social Concerns, edited by William H. Shannon. New York: Farrar, Straus and Giroux, 1985.

Honorable Reader: Reflections on My Work, edited by Robert E. Daggy. New York: Crossroad, 1989.

The Inner Experience: Notes on Contemplation, edited by William H. Shannon. New York: Harper Collins, 2004.

Love and Living, edited by Naomi Burton Stone and Patrick Hart. New York: Farrar, Straus and Giroux, 1979.

New Seeds of Contemplation. New York: New Directions, 1961.

No Man Is an Island. New York: Harcourt Brace, 1955.

The Road to Joy: Letters to New and Old Friends, edited by Robert E. Daggy. New York: Farrar, Straus and Giroux, 1989.

The Sign of Jonas. New York: Harcourt Brace, 1953.

Spiritual Direction and Meditation. Wheathampstead, Herts.: Anthony Clarke, 1975.

A Vow of Conversation: Journals 1964–1965, edited by Naomi Burton Stone. New York: Farrar, Straus and Giroux, 1988.

The Waters of Siloe. New York: Harcourt Brace, 1949.

The Wisdom of the Desert. New York: New Directions, 1960.